The King of Football

The Story of Pelé

Tony Bradman

Contents

OXFORD
UNIVERSITY PRESS

Great Clarendon Street, Oxford OX2 6DP

Oxford University Press is a department of the University of Oxford.
It furthers the University's objective of excellence in research, scholarship, and education by publishing worldwide in

Oxford New York

Auckland Cape Town Dar es Salaam Hong Kong Karachi
Kuala Lumpur Madrid Melbourne Mexico City Nairobi
New Delhi Shanghai Taipei Toronto

With Offices in

Argentina Austria Brazil Chile Czech Republic France
Greece Guatemala Hungary Italy Japan Poland Portugal
Singapore South Korea Switzerland Thailand Turkey
Ukraine Vietnam

First published 2003

British Library Cataloguing in Publication Data

Data available

ISBN 13: 978 0 19 919538 1
ISBN 10: 0 19 919538 2

10 9 8 7 6 5

True Stories Pack 2 (one of each title)
ISBN 13: 978 0 19 919545 9
ISBN 10: 0 19 919545 5
True Stories Pack 2 Class Pack (six of each title)
ISBN 13: 978 0 19 919544 2
ISBN 10: 0 19 919544 7

Acknowledgements

The publisher would like to thank the following for permission to reproduce photographs:

Associated Press: pp 3, 29, 30; Corbis/Leonard de Selva: p 21;
Empics: p 8; Mirrorpix; p 19

Front cover background photo: Associated Press
Inset photo: Empics
Back cover: Empics

Illustrations are by Trevor Parkin

Printed in Great Britain by Ashford Colour Press, Gosport, Hants

Introduction

This is the story of a boy who grew up to be a great footballer. His name is Pelé, and he was born in Brazil. He played in four World Cups between 1958 and 1970 and he is probably the most famous footballer ever.

This is how it all happened …

Chapter 1

Pelé's Dream

It all started in 1940 when Pelé was born in a small village.

Pelé's father was a **professional footballer**, but a serious **injury** meant that he never made much money from the game. So Pelé's family was quite poor.

Pelé did lots of jobs to help his parents. But he also played football in the streets with his friends.

He decided he wanted to be a footballer like his father. Pelé's mother didn't like the idea.

Chapter 2

Pelé Plays for Santos

Nothing was going to stop Pelé making his dream come true.

He played for several local teams, then at the age of 15 he was given a **trial** by a big club called Santos. He was very talented, and Santos took him on.

Pelé's mother cried when Pelé told her. It meant her son would have to leave home to live in the city.

Pelé was homesick too. But he stuck it out, and he soon had his reward. He scored a goal in his first game for the team.

Chapter 3

Pelé – "The Black Pearl"

It was the first goal of many. Within a year, Pelé had scored 32 goals for his club.

Pelé with the Santos team

Then he was chosen to play for his country, Brazil. In his first two **international games**, he scored three goals.

Soon football fans started calling him "The Black Pearl".

Pelé was still only 16. There was a World Cup coming up in Sweden, and he wondered if he would be picked for the team.

He listened closely when the players were **announced** on the radio … he had to sit down when he heard his name!

Pelé was 17 when he arrived in Sweden in 1958. He was the youngest player in the Brazilian team. He was quite small for a footballer, and very skinny, but everyone was expecting great things from him.

Chapter 4

Pelé's First World Cup

Pelé had a knee injury, and he didn't play until Brazil's third game, against the Soviet Union. But he scored a goal in the next match against Wales, a 1–0 win.

Then, in the semi-final game against France, Pelé scored a brilliant **hat-trick** – three goals in one game!

Thanks to Pelé, his country's team was in the World Cup Final.

Chapter 5

Champions of the World!

Brazil were playing against Sweden. The game started badly for Brazil – Sweden were leading, 1–0. But before long Brazil were 2–1 in the lead. Then, in the second half, Pelé scored twice.

In the end Brazil won 5–2 – they were the champions of the world!

Pelé's team mates carried him round the pitch on their shoulders. It was a wonderful moment.

But there were troubles ahead …

Chapter 6

Injury

Pelé became famous all around the world. He travelled to many countries with Santos. He played almost 100 matches a year. It was very tiring and very hard on the body of a young player.

Then in the 1962 World Cup in Chile, Pelé played in the first game, but he was injured in the second.

Now he was out of the **tournament**.

Pelé watched sadly as Brazil went on to win the cup without him. He wondered if he would ever play for Brazil again.

Pelé had a tough time in the 1966 World Cup.

Pelé did recover, and he did play for Brazil again in the World Cup in England in 1966. But everything went wrong for Brazil and for Pelé. He became injured again and was **fouled** time after time. Brazil lost – they were out.

England won the final, but a sad Pelé was already back in Brazil.

Chapter 7

Goal 1000!

This time Pelé was so tired he said he would never play in another World Cup. He knew he would always be a target for the hard men in other teams, and he didn't want to be badly hurt.

For a while, Pelé thought that football might have lost its magic …

A Brazilian stamp featuring Pelé

But Pelé's love of the game was bound to return. He kept playing for Santos, and he kept scoring goals.

Then, in 1969, he hit the net for the 1000th time! Pelé was 29, a married man with children, and now the most famous and important player on Earth.

Another World Cup was coming up in Mexico in 1970. Pelé was asked to play, and he almost said no. Then he changed his mind and said yes. He felt he still had something to prove.

Lots of people said he couldn't play in a World Cup without getting injured. Pelé wanted to show that they were wrong. He knew it was going to be difficult.

There were several very strong teams in it. England were the world champions, and the Italian team looked very tough.

Chapter 8

Pelé Comes Back

The Brazilian team spent three months together in a training camp, and everybody worked hard.

Pelé couldn't wait for the tournament to begin …

Brazil did well. They won against five countries, including England. Now they were to play in the final – against Italy!

Over 107,000 people crammed into the Azteca **Stadium** in Mexico City to watch the game – and 600 million people round the world watched it on television.

Brazil attacked from the **kick-off**, but the Italian team seemed very strong. Then Pelé hit a powerful header past the Italian keeper. Brazil were 1–0 up, and it seemed nothing could stop them from winning the cup now.

But the Brazilian team gave away a stupid goal – the score was 1–1 …

Brazil soon came back, though. They scored a second goal, then Pelé set up another goal for one of his team mates.

But the best goal was the last. Pelé had the ball, and his captain, Carlos Alberto, was steaming up on his right. Pelé waited till the last moment, then made a brilliant pass to Carlos Alberto who blasted the ball into the back of the net.

Brazil 4, Italy 1!

Pelé never played in another World Cup and retired as a player in 1977.

He is still involved in the sport and does lots of charity work around the world.

Pelé supporting a children's charity

Chapter 9

Pelé – the King of Football!

But no one will ever forget the day in Mexico when Brazil won the World Cup for the third time – and showed that football could be a beautiful game.

And at the heart of the greatest team was the greatest player – Pelé – the man the Brazilians call *o rei* – the King of Football!

Celebrations after winning the 1970 World Cup

Glossary

announce to tell people about something special

foul an unfair tackle on an opposition player

hat-trick when one player scores three goals in a single game

injury damage to any part of your body

international game a game between two different countries

kick-off when one team starts a game by kicking the ball

professional footballer someone who gets paid to play football

stadium a football pitch with seats around it so lots of people can watch a game

tournament a competition where lots of teams compete to win a cup

trial a test game to see which players are good

Index